WHERE DiD VAN GOGH GO?

Written by
SATU HÄMEENHAO-FOX

Illustrated by
LÉONIE DESPRÉS

Katsushika Hokusai (1760-1849)

Katsushika Hokusai was an engraver and printmaker in the Edo region of Japan (modern-day Tokyo). He made thousands of prints and even drew illustrations for a series of adventure stories. His most well-known series of prints was of Japan's famous volcano, Mount Fuji, and included *The Great Wave*.

The artist

Vincent van Gogh

2

The Great Wave
Hokusai's most famous painting of Mount Fuji includes a huge wave.

Cranes
Elegant cranes feature in several Hokusai prints.

Samurai
Hokusai created prints of fierce warriors wearing elaborate armor.

Child and kite
Hokusai often showed kite-flying in his *Mount Fuji* print series.

Lady and parasol
Hokusai featured elegant sunshades in prints like *Girl with Parasol*.

James Van Der Zee (1886-1983)

James Van Der Zee was a photographer who lived in Harlem, New York. In the 1910s, he established a studio where people could come to have a great photo taken. Van Der Zee took pride in making his customers look their best. He even photographed famous people, including political activists and artists.

The artist

Vincent van Gogh

World War I soldier
Van Der Zee took photos of soldiers returning from war.

Glamorous couple
Van Der Zee's photos captured successful Black Americans during the Harlem Renaissance.

Basketball player
Sports teams came to Van Der Zee's studio for group portraits.

Music school
Van Der Zee's sister Jennie ran a music school or "conservatory."

Hazel Scott
Van Der Zee photographed this musician and activist.

Giovanni Canaletto (1697-1768)

Giovanni Canaletto began his career painting scenery for plays in his father's workshop. Over time, he started painting the city where he lived: Venice, Italy. The city has hundreds of canals, and people often get around by boat. To this day, thousands of tourists visit Venice every day. In the 18th century, tourists could buy a Canaletto painting as a souvenir.

The artist

Vincent van Gogh

Bridge
he Rialto is a covered
bridge in Venice. It
is the oldest canal
bridge in Venice.

Carnival mask
Masks were worn
during the annual
Carnival celebrations.

Opera poster
Canaletto painted
scenes for operas,
sometimes with
his father.

Luggage
Tourists in the 18th
century needed
luggage on holiday,
just like us!

The Duke's barge
The Duke of Venice's
barge features in
Canaletto's painting of
the annual "Marriage
of the Sea" ceremony.

Georgia O'Keeffe (1887-1986)

In 1929, the painter Georgia O'Keeffe visited New Mexico and fell in love with the dry desert landscape. She set up home in a place called "Ghost Ranch" and painted many works of art inspired by the natural world she saw around her. She also painted images of flowers very close up, as if she looked at them through a magnifying glass.

The artist

Vincent van Gogh

Cow's skull
O'Keeffe painted bleached animal bones.

Bo and Chia
The painter had two fluffy Chow Chow dogs.

Alfred Stieglitz
O'Keeffe's husband was a photographer.

Jimsonweed
O'Keeffe liked Jimsonweed plants, even though they are poisonous.

Roadrunner
The roadrunner is the official state bird of New Mexico.

Henri Rousseau (1844-1910)

Henri Rousseau lived in Paris, France, but he dreamed up lush, tropical locations for his paintings. To find inspiration, he walked around the city's botanical gardens. Rousseau was a busy man—in addition to painting and spending time with his many artist friends he had several jobs, including as a tax collector and playing the violin.

The artist

Vincent van Gogh

Tiger
Rousseau loved painting big cats. This tiger sprang up in the painting *Surprised!*

Lion
Another big cat can be seen in the painting *The Repast of the Lion*.

Sonia Delauney
Delauney was one of Rousseau's many friends from the art world.

Musician
Rousseau painted fellow musicians. This one plays the mandolin.

Scrapbook
As a joke, Rousseau collected his bad reviews in a scrapbook.

Nellie Mae Rowe (1900-1982)

Nellie Mae Rowe lived in Vinings, Georgia, USA. As a young girl, she made dolls from the clothes she found in the laundry basket. Rowe turned her whole home into a work of art (art that spans a large area is called "installation art.") Her colorful home became famous, and people would visit the great artist in her "Playhouse."

The artist

Vincent van Gogh

Chewing gum
Rowe created sculptures from everyday materials such as gum.

Dog
Images of vibrantly colored pets featured in Rowe's works.

Doll
Rowe's earliest sculptures were handmade dolls.

Chair
Rowe included an empty chair in several paintings, such as *Nellie's Birthday*.

Art materials
Pencils and crayons were used by Rowe to achieve vivid colors in her works.

Salvador Dalí (1904-1989)

Salvador Dalí studied art in the bustling Spanish city of Madrid. He began by copying famous paintings at the city's art gallery, but he is most famous for his surreal paintings and sculptures. Surreal art mixes surprising things together to create an unexpected image with a deeper meaning. He went on to create surreal works like *Lobster Telephone* and even published a surrealist cookbook.

The artist

Vincent van Gogh

Lobster phone
Dalí made sculptures by putting together unlikely objects.

Ocelot
Dalí had a pet ocelot—a kind of big cat.

Butterfly eyes
This unusual butterfly was painted by Dalí for a book cover.

Shoe hat
Dalí created this hat with designer Elsa Schiaparelli.

Melting clock
This strange timepiece is in Dalí's painting *The Persistence of Memory.*

Adélaïde Labille-Guiard (1749-1803)

The French painter Adélaïde Labille-Guiard lived through the French Revolution. She painted portraits of the royal family and was one of very few women allowed into the Academy, the exclusive club for painters in Paris. Labille-Guiard was also a teacher of art and a champion of women artists.

The artist

Vincent van Gogh

Parrot
Labille-Guiard included her sitters' rare and exotic pets in their portraits.

Fire
Some of Labille-Guiard's paintings were burned during the French Revolution.

Necklace
The lady wearing these gems was the queen of France, Marie Antoinette.

Pamphlet
Critics of Labille-Guiard wrote pamphlets saying women shouldn't be painters.

Robespierre
Maximilien Robespierre was the leader of the French Revolution.

Florine Stettheimer (1871-1944)

Florine Stettheimer loved painting her home city of New York. Her most famous paintings are of the city's landmarks, such as the museums, the financial district on Wall Street, the shopping street Fifth Avenue, and Broadway. Broadway was—and still is—a bustling collection of theaters where plays and musicals are performed.

The artist

Vincent van Gogh

Broadway show
Stettheimer painted theaters in her work *The Cathedrals of Broadway*.

Ballet dancer
Stettheimer was influenced by the famous dance company the Ballets Russes.

Pekingese
This dog appeared in one of Stettheimer's paintings of a sale at a department store.

Movie theater
During the Jazz Age, which Stettheimer painted, movie theaters would often also have stage shows.

Statue of Liberty
Stettheimer painted this New York landmark in her work *New York/Liberty*.

Vincent van Gogh (1853-1890)

Home at last! During his time in Arles, France, Van Gogh painted small objects like a chair or a vase of sunflowers. He was also inspired to paint outside and produced images of starry nights and the wind blowing through the trees. These images of ordinary life were turned into something special through his use of color. Like all the artists in this book, Van Gogh is loved around the world for making works of art that are unique to him.

The artist

Yellow paint
Van Gogh used rare Indian yellow paint for painting stars.

Potatoes
Van Gogh painted local villagers peeling, cooking, and eating potatoes in his painting *The Potato Eaters*.

The Red Vineyard
This painting of farmers harvesting is the only one Van Gogh sold in his lifetime.

Chair
Van Gogh made paintings of his furniture.

Postman
Van Gogh exchanged many letters with his brother Theo.

Sunflowers
The painting *Sunflowers* has become one the world's most famous works of art.

Katsushika Hokusai (1760–1849)

 The artist

 Vincent van Gogh

 The Great Wave

 Cranes

 Samurai

 Child and kite

 Lady and parasol

Edo period Japan (p. 2–3)

Under the Wave off Kanagawa (Kanagawa oki nami ura), also known as *The Great Wave*, from the series *Thirty-six Views of Mount Fuji (Fugaku sanjūrokkei)*
Created: ca. 1830–32

Hokusai played with perspective to create this piece in which the wave looks like it is about to break over Mount Fuji, a famous volcano in Japan. He was famous for his use of the color "Prussian blue," seen in this print.

James Van Der Zee (1886–1983)

 The artist

 Vincent van Gogh

 World War I soldier

 Glamorous couple

 Basketball player

 Music school

 Hazel Scott

The Harlem Renaissance (p. 4–5)

Couple, Harlem
Created: 1932

In this photograph, a couple pose in their fur coats with their Cadillac car. Van Der Zee's photography chronicled the lives of Black people in New York City during the Harlem Renaissance and beyond.

Giovanni Canaletto (1697–1768)

The artist

Vincent van Gogh

The bridge

Carnival mask

Opera poster

Luggage

The Duke's barge

Busy and bustling Venice (p. 6–7)

The Grand Canal, Venice, Looking South toward the Rialto Bridge
Created: 1730s

This oil painting shows the largest canal in Venice. Canals are waterways that people in Venice use to travel around on boats called gondolas. This painting is one of 20 works of the same size.

Georgia O'Keeffe (1887–1986)

The artist

Vincent van Gogh

Cow's skull

Bo and Chia

Alfred Stieglitz

Jimsonweed

Roadrunner

Dramatic New Mexico (p. 8–9)
Black Place II
Created: 1944

"The Black Place" is a real location: a landscape near O'Keeffe's home in New Mexico. This oil painting is inspired by the place where two hills meet at The Black Place.

Henri Rousseau (1844–1910)

 The artist

 Vincent van Gogh

 Tiger

 Lion

 Sonia Delauney

 Musician

 Scrapbook

Jungle at dawn (p. 10–11)

The Repast of the Lion
Created: ca. 1907

When Rousseau painted this image of a lion eating its prey, he was inspired by the exotic plants of Paris' botanical gardens and animals he had seen in children's books.

Nellie Mae Rowe (1900–1982)

The artist

Vincent van Gogh

Chewing gum

Dog

Doll

Chair

Art materials

A colorful birthday (p. 12–13)

Nellie's Birthday
Created: 1981

Rowe made this pencil and crayon drawing to celebrate her own birthday. It mixes both real and fanciful objects. Rowe's art often features a Tree of Life, and one can be seen on the top left of this piece.

27

Salvador Dalí (1904–1989)

The artist	Vincent van Gogh	Lobster phone	Ocelot	Butterfly eyes	Shoe hat	Melting clock

Strange and surreal (p. 14–15)

Publisher's proof for the cover of Maurice Sandoz, 'La Limite' (Paris 1951)
Created: 1950

As well as painting, Dalí created many illustrations for books. This image was created for the cover of a book by a Swiss author named Maurice Sandoz.

Adélaïde Labille-Guiard (1749–1803)

The artist   **Vincent van Gogh**   **Parrot**   **Fire**   **Necklace**   **Pamphlet**   **Robespierre**

Art education (p. 16–17)
Self-Portrait with Two Pupils, Marie Gabrielle Capet (1761-1818) and Marie Marguerite Carraux de Rosemond (1765-1788)
Created: 1785

This oil painting shows the artist herself and two students. Labille-Guiard has painted herself in elegant—but impractical—clothing. Many artists in the 18th century would do this when making self-portraits.

Florine Stettheimer (1871–1944)

The artist

Vincent van Gogh

Broadway show

Ballet dancer

Pekingese

Movie theater

Statue of Liberty

New York City lights (p. 18–19)

The Cathedrals of Art
Created: 1942

This painting was one of a series of four. Each painting in the series shows an element of New York life. This one contains references to the city's art galleries and museums, including The Metropolitan Museum of Art.

Vincent van Gogh (1853–1890)

The artist

Yellow paint

Potatoes

The Red Vineyard

Chair

Postman

Sunflowers

French country life (p. 20–21)
Self-Portrait with a Straw Hat
(obverse: *The Potato Peeler*)
Created: 1887

Van Gogh painted more than 20 self-portraits between 1886 and 1888. He couldn't afford to pay a model to sit for him, so instead he bought a mirror and painted his own portrait. On the other side of the canvas is a painting of a peasant.

Project Editor Vicky Armstrong
Senior Designer Nathan Martin
Production Editor Siu Yin Chan
Senior Production Controller Louise Minihane
Senior Acquisitions Editor Katy Flint
Design Manager Vicky Short
Managing Director Mark Searle

Designed for DK by Zoë Tucker

First American Edition, 2024
Published in the United States by DK Publishing,
a Division of Penguin Random House LLC
1745 Broadway, 20th Floor, New York, NY 10019

24 25 26 27 28 10 9 8 7 6 5 4 3 2 1
001–340067–Nov/2024

A catalog record for this book is available from the Library of Congress.
ISBN 978-0-7440-9889-1

DK books are available at special discounts when purchased in bulk
for sales promotions, premiums, fund-raising, or educational use.
For details, contact: DK Publishing Special Markets,
1745 Broadway, 20th Floor, New York, NY 10019
SpecialSales@dk.com

Printed and bound in Slovakia
www.dk.com

DK would like to thank The Metropolitan Museum of Art for their kind
permission to reproduce images of artworks from their collection.

22: *Under the Wave off Kanagawa (Kanagawa oki nami ura)*, also known as *The Great Wave*, from the series *Thirty-six Views of Mount Fuji (Fugaku sanjūrokkei)* (ca. 1930-32) by Katsushika Hokusai. Japanese. JP1847 (br). **23:** *Couple, Harlem* (1932, printed later) by James Van Der Zee. American. 2021.446.1.2 © James Van Der Zee Archive, The Metropolitan Museum of Art (br). **24:** *The Grand Canal, Venice, Looking South toward the Rialto Bridge* (1730s) by Giovanni Canaletto. Italian. 2019.141.2 (br). **25:** *Black Place II* (1944) by Georgia O'Keeffe. American. 59.204.1 (br). **26:** *The Repast of the Lion* (ca. 1907) by Henri Rousseau. French. 51.112.5 (br). **27:** *Nellie's Birthday* (1981) by Nellie Mae Rowe. American. 2014.548.31 Gift of Souls Grown Deep Foundation from the William S. Arnett Collection, 2014 / © ARS, NY and DACS, London 2024 / © DACS 2024 (br). **28:** *Publisher's proof for the cover of Maurice Sandoz, 'La Limite' (Paris 1951)* (1950) by Salvador Dalí. Spanish. 50.627 © Salvador Dali, Fundació Gala-Salvador Dalí, DACS 2024 / © DACS 2024 (br). **29:** *Self-Portrait with Two Pupils, Marie Gabrielle Capet (1761-1818) and Marie Marguerite Carraux de Rosemond (1765-1788)* (1785) by Adélaïde Labille-Guiard. French. 53.225.5 (br). **30:** *The Cathedrals of Art* (1942) by Florine Stettheimer. American. 53.24.1 (br). **31:** *Self-Portrait with a Straw Hat (obverse: The Potato Peeler)* (1887) by Vincent Van Gogh. Dutch. 67.187.70a (br).